She's had her heart broken countless times...
Yet every time she falls in love
She still believes it's going to last forever

She's so grateful for every painful step of her journey
Appreciating that...

Every broken heart has left cracks for more light to enter
Every love story has written another chapter of her life
Every scar is there to remind her of her beauty
Every dark night has ended with a sunrise
Every tear has reflected her infinite light
Every heartache has taught her more about love

She forgives easily
She loves deeply
She regrets nothing

Her depth is infinite
Her religion is love
Her poetry is straight from the heart.

Thank you to all the men who hurt me over the years...

Thank you for mirroring my wounds
Thank you for reflecting my fears
Thank you for releasing my expectations
Thank you for loosening my attachments

Thank you for teaching me acceptance
Thank you for pushing me to see my pain
Thank you for helping me to surrender to flow
Thank you for showing me how to love myself

Thank you for forcing me to redefine love
Thank you for walking this journey with me
Thank you for breaking my heart...

Enough to let the light in.

Karen Star

And Then I Met You

Austin Macauley Publishers™
LONDON • CAMBRIDGE • NEW YORK • SHARJAH

A CIP catalogue record for this title is available from the
British Library.

ISBN 9781528904247 (Paperback)
ISBN 9781528957649 (ePub e-book)

www.austinmacauley.com

First Published (2019)
Austin Macauley Publishers Ltd
25 Canada Square
Canary Wharf
London
E14 5LQ

Acknowledgements

Heartfelt gratitude to Yukia Azorah Sandara for the light-encoded cover design of this book.

Yukia, as a Divine Sound Alchemist, Light Language Speaker and Quantum Light Code Artist, has the ability to bring in divine frequencies of ancient light language, spoken and written.

These codes recalibrate the human energy field to be able to hold higher vibrations of love and light, which are essential for building our luminous light body and to sustain very high levels of frequency in our New Earth.

Table of Contents

Part 1
Yearning

Rising in love
From the Ocean of Chaos
She awaited the One
Who would fearlessly ride
Her tidal wave to Heaven.

Butterflies

Something's started stirring
From deep inside my heart
Our song is playing butterflies
Beating in unison from afar

In the silence I can hear you
Angels singing from above
Joyful symphony of the cosmos
Reuniting sacred love.

Dream Man

He don't exist, her demons snickered
Laughing in her face
That one you call your dream man
A ploy, to keep the boys away

But as she sleepily closed her eyes
Her anticipation grew
She awaited the thumping of her heart
To know his love was true

He gently took her by the hand
Off they flew into the night
Exploring distant galaxies
Skinny-dipping in starlight

They danced in the rain on Jupiter
Recited Rumi on Neptune
Kissed in the fires of Venus
And picnicked on the moon

Before tucking her back in bed
He stole one final kiss
And while he never showed his face
The love she felt was bliss

Awakening with the sunlight
She knew they were never apart
For her dream man was safe at home
In the chambers of her heart.

Symphony of the Cosmos

The symphony of the cosmos
Is dancing with me
Silent flow of the music
Love breaking hearts free

Pulsing drum beat of blood
Ignites fire in my breath
Surrendering to the rhythm
Freeing minds to forget

I hear you laughing nearby
Feel your song fill my heart
Once our music aligns
We'll be dancing on Earth.

Homesick

She was homesick for her planet
Memories of a distant galaxy
Where love's pure vibration
Sings its heavenly melody

Recalling their final dance
Before the journey down to Earth
You'll know it's me, he whispered
Your love will open up my heart

He promised he would find her
And she'd know he was the one
Hearing the music of the cosmos
When he kissed her with his song

Men came and said they loved her
But wouldn't let her see inside
Their hearts locked up in cages
Afraid to let their depth run wild

So she sleeps under the stars
It's where she feels closest to home
Until he finds her once again
And they can dance their sacred tune.

Dreamtime

I can smell your passion rising
In the heat of the night
Tasting your lips melting
Oh such soft, sweet delight

Hearing your heart pounding
Urgent rhythms of desire
Seeing our love burning
Eyes engulfed in sacred fire

Touching your soul gently
Kisses dancing down your spine
Breathing timeless moments
As our bodies lay entwined

Knowing I'm in Heaven
We are forever here as one
Forgetting that when dawn breaks
My dreams will all be gone.

Good Morning Kisses

With passion on her mind
She felt her beating heart
Fired up with burning love
Brighter than the stars

The angels felt her yearning
Flying in a precious gift
It can be anything you choose dear
Close your eyes and make a wish

Well she didn't want no diamonds
When she had them in the sky
And all the rubies she desired
Were flowering in the valley nearby

She knew she needed nothing
Yet she felt something was missing
Good morning kisses, she laughed
That would be the sweetest blessing

As she opened her gift from Heaven
Stars danced inside her heart
For the only present she ever wanted
Was to wake up in his arms.

Goodnight Angel

There's a place where I meet you
Between awake and half asleep
When my heart it starts racing
And your presence demands to speak

As you wrap your wings around me
I know you've come to say goodnight
Shifting from the world of our dreams
Into an angel by my side.

Heartbeat

Echoing the silence of the night
Our hearts dancing to the beat
Thumping footsteps to the rhythm
Awakening me again from my sleep

Cosmic music that we share
Is so much more than just a dream
Feeling the murmurs of your soul
Whispering sweet nothings in my ear

The raw power of our dance
Is enough for me to know
Your thoughts are here with me
Our love will always grow

Joyful lovers of the night
Kissing in amongst the stars
Soulful music of the cosmos
Reuniting sacred hearts.

Heartstrings

No need for words
Just focus on your heart
Where our truth does the talking
We can never be apart

I feel you always there
In that space filled with love
The sweetest ache of knowing
Tells us more than enough

The music that we share
Pumping blood to the beat
Sacred rhythm of the lovers
Slow dancing in the heat

Thumping deep into the night
It's when I know I'm on your mind
Our hearts forever whispering
Heavenly words from the Divine.

Glorious Mess

Her body moved to write a love song
To the one who would want to stay
The man who could tune her heartstrings
Without changing the music she played

He never asked that she sing any louder
Or dim her dance into anything less
To him she was always enough
Just expressing her glorious mess.

Heaven

There's a place in my heart
A sacred room just for one
To be cherished and adored
As my beloved divine man

This is my intimate space
Where I share all of my being
My body, its secrets
Deepest desires and feelings

Gently wrapped up in love
But with the freedom to fly
Surrendering deeper to heights
Soaring together we'll rise

A safe haven to bravely
Knock down our walls
Opening together in bliss
A soft landing to fall

But if you ever decide
To move out of Heaven
Through my tears I will kiss you
And give you my blessings.

Midnight

How can I sleep
With you here lying next to me
Yet I can't see you
Or touch you
My heart knows what it feels

Longing to see your face
I know soon all will be revealed
You will find me here
On Earth
Divinity unfolding sacred deals

Escapades throughout the night
Lost in the magic of your charms
But please hold me
Just for now
So I can fall asleep in your arms.

Divine Intimacy

In the silence she could hear him
Speaking softly to her heart
The power of love so finely tuned
Whispering from afar

As she listened a little closer
She felt his divine intimacy
Tingles dancing down her spine
Met the music of his kisses

The symphony of the cosmos
Heard only by their hearts
Sweet words of love he sang for her
Forever written in the stars.

Sleepless

When I can't sleep
Does that mean
You are thinking of me?
Wrapping me tight in your arms
Till I can no longer breathe

Feeling the beat of your heart
Drumming love up my spine
Your fingers reaching to touch
Each awakened curve of desire

Tasting my scent on your skin
As our bodies entwine
Wide awake on the dance floor
Losing control of my mind

As I bathe in your light
Slipping from my world to yours
Floating on pillows of dreams
As sweet surrender unfurls

Begging for sleep in a land
Where love is always alive
You whisper
Close your eyes now darling
I'll wake you up at sunrise.

Yearning

She yearns to be seen by his silence
She dreams to be heard by his smile
She wants to be felt by his words
She longs to be touched by his eyes

She craves to be opened by his presence
She hungers to be melted by his fire
She burns to be possessed by his trust
She thirsts to be tasted by his desire

She aches to be kissed by his depth
She lusts to be devoured by his strength
She demands to be ravished by his heart
She surrenders to be penetrated by love.

Part 2
Loving

With a head full of poetry
And a heart filled with love
Just breathing with him
Was enough.

Afterglow

When the music is gone
And the silence unfolds
The dance of the lovers
Truths naked, exposed

Raw love is the moment
When all is revealed
Light gently surrendering
What we seek to conceal

Entwined in the spotlight
All pretence falls apart
In the sound of your breath
And the beat of my heart.

Burning

You slipped into my world
In the space between breaths
Blazing a trail to my heart
With every tremor we felt

Murmuring lyrics from Heaven
Moments dripped in desire
Bodies melting with passion
Battles lost in our sighs

We surrendered to love
As the walls tumbled down
Eternity glimpsed in the flames
Sacred warriors on fire

And now as I lay here
Breathing each moment in time
Your touch is still burning
Heartstrings forever entwined.

Unleashed Passion

This is the shell he loved to smash
That refined aloofness
She presented to the outside world

He revelled in opening the portal
To her divine wilderness
Knowing she had chosen him
Above all others
To expose her vulnerable softness

Forever lost
In the reservoir
Of unleashed passion

She reserved just for him.

Committed to Love

I cannot commit myself to you
Yet we can both commit to love
Could never promise you eternity
But we can promise love us

For in our co-created world
Where timelines are shifting
Freedom together in unity
Flight of true love existing

So come now and kiss me
Melt your lips into mine
Two hearts fusing together
Forever moments in time.

Fusion

Lying here naked
Writing poetry on your skin
Wondering where is it I end
And where do you begin?

Fingers tracing love letters
Slowly down your spine
Goosebumps quivering with joy
As your world collides with mine

Breath dancing to the rhythm
Hearts drumming sacred beats
Heaven rejoicing in our sighs
Bodies melting in the heat

Without a beginning or an end
There is no you or me
Lost forever in this moment
Surrendering to love to set us free.

Daisy Chain

I can only promise to love you now
For tomorrow may never come
Moments are like a daisy chain
Linked together in the sun

Each daisy picked eventually dies
But the sun still shines its light
New flowers blooming all the time
Colours dancing oh so bright

So take your nows and make a crown
Fill your heart with flowering love
Live with joy, it's free for all
Timeless moments in the sun.

Falling

She woke up with the Angels
Balancing her on the edge
Tonight you learn to fly my dear
Be brave and take the risk

Fear tightening her heartstrings
The unknown echoing its call
Raw memories of crash landings
Scars of men who'd let her fall

As the Angels bid farewell
They reminded her of her wings
The key you seek to flight
Is in the faith that you are free

Peering deep into the void
She swallowed down her screams
Was he waiting there as promised?
Or just another ruptured dream?

Unlocking the secret to her power
She beheld the hunger to believe
Fearlessly stretching out her wings
She surrendered to the breeze

Hurtling through the darkness
She felt him take her by the hand
There's no need for me to catch you
When I'm here, flying by your side.

Found

Love is never lost
It just isn't found
Hidden in the illusion
Of darkness in our minds

The pain that we are feeling
Light blown out within our hearts
Plunging life into the darkness
Blanketing promises from the stars

Change is the only constant
Sweet surrender to the flow
Following roads which lead to peace
Allowing love to always grow

So open up the curtains
And let the sunshine stream on in
Live each moment as in Heaven
And always choose to let love win.

Kisses in the Wind

Love letters posted in the wind
Arrived upon my shores today
Your kisses blowing in the breeze
Sent from a million miles away

Gusts wrapping arms around me
I feel your breath upon my lips
Fingers running through my hair
Sighs tasting every kiss

Goosebumps rising on my skin
Shivers dancing down my spine
Sacred moments sent from Heaven
Defying Earthly space and time

Your presence howling in my ears
Embracing freedom with its roar
Symphonies blasting through the air
Hearts dancing as we soar

Then whispering that you loved me
You reminded me of one last thing
That whenever I was missing you
To feel your kisses in the wind.

Kisses to Heaven

How will you kiss me?
She needed to know
Unbridled with passion
Or deliciously slow?

Tasting your love song
From your lips to mine
Bodies slow dancing
Heartstrings entwined

Moments lost in forever
In a world with no time
Your kiss is my Heaven
Your sweet surrender
Through mine.

Moonlight

Their hearts they danced together
Like leaves frolicking in the breeze
Free to float up to the Heavens
Content to tiptoe through the trees

It was there under the moonlight
His love wiped her tears away
As she surrendered to the rhythm
Angel harps began to play

So whichever way the wind blows
She knows it's written in the stars
Their song will dance forever more
To the beating of their hearts.

Sacred Space

A direct path to Heaven
Can be found easily enough
Once we knock down our walls
Laying down our defences

Feeling your love fill my heart
Returning the abundance to you
Safe in our sanctuary of trust
Unwrapping the present of truth

Sweet love that is flowing
Between your heart and mine
Creating that pure, sacred space
To become one with the Divine.

Seduced

I'm gonna undress your heart
And strip bare your soul
Seduced by your light
As your colours unfold

Caress every inch
Of your naked reveal
Kissing each scar
That you seek to conceal

Make love to your smile
As your eyes dance with mine
Delighting
Exciting
Bodies entwined

As we surrender to love
There is no more to do
For your truth is in me
And I am now you.

Love Shack

Well she didn't need no penthouse
Just a love shack on the beach
With a garden filled with butterflies
Warm sand massaging her feet

And she didn't want no diamonds
Just the sparkling nighttime sky
With a rooftop filled with passion
Moonlight dancing in his eyes

Coz she didn't have no promises
Just the presents of today
Hearts filled with love and laughter
Priceless gifts to give away.

True Love

Our divine love is your freedom
My present given each day
Your choice to surrender to Heaven
Or drift further away

If your joy dances with us
Or heart yearns for another
True love seeks only your bliss
The sacred gift between lovers.

Wild Seeds

How did you find your way into my heart?
I was already there, dear, right from the start
We made our agreement before coming to Earth
To plant my seeds wild in the depths of your world

Struggling through darkness I reached for your light
Basking in sunshine I accepted your night
Twisting roots deeper I weathered your storms
Drinking sweet nectar I made love to your thorns

Hearts opening to bridge divine portals to Heaven
Flowers blossoming as love draws us closer together
Light painting rainbows to each beat of our song
Your scent kissing the air and carrying me home.

Part 3
Feeling

Wild hearts
Cannot be caged
We need to be free
To love without limits.

All or Nothing

When I fall in love with you
There can't be no half measures
It's got to be all or nothing
All the pain and all the pleasures

For feeling is the greatest gift
Without it how am I to know
If I'm surrendering to the depths of love
Or battling defiantly against the flow

Both pain and joy are gifts you see
Whispered guidance from above
Divine messages from our hearts
Reminding us to always align with love.

Angel Song

I cried the day you told me
You'd lost your little girl
The cruellest cut that slashed your heart
Bleeding darkness in your world

She's coming through me now
She wants to say hello
To tell you of the reasons why
She felt the need to go

Daddy, up here I'm an angel
My world is filled with peace and love
Hearts wide open, no more pain
Singing harmonies with the doves

I know you are still hurting
But it's what we chose to do
Your strength is in the love you feel
Divine light will pull you through

So as I hold you in my arms
Allow your tears their sweet release
Surrender to my angel song
And let your heart be filled with peace.

Believe

You tell me you love me
But why is that so?
Why do you love me?
How do you know?

You say love is forever
Yet can I believe?
How do I trust you?
That love will just be?

Come here my dear
Lay your head on my heart
Hear my truth speaking
Feel light lift the dark

Love does not speak
In reasons or rhymes
It doesn't have answers
Or need to know why

Asking logic to find
A reason to love you
Just gives me a reason
To love you no more

So now do you see
How that just cannot be
Love is felt in the heart
Not the mind or the thoughts

Love's reason is love
What more do you need?
And that there is our Heaven
If you dare to believe.

Serenaded

The rain soaked her
Pouring down his love
So she hid inside the cave
Until she felt the emptiness

The sun awakened her
Lighting up his passion
So she dived into the ocean
Until she found the darkness

The wind teased her
Calling out his name
So she ran into the forest
Until she heard the silence

Amidst the calmness of the storm
Rain washed away her tears
Sun melted her defences
Wind swept away her fears

The symphony of the cosmos
Eternally serenading her with stars
Until she could no longer ignore
The silent tug of his heart.

Drifting

If I'm hurting it's because
I've become too attached
Headaches pounding a future
My mind trapped in the past

I know I have to let go
To surrender all thoughts
Release every expectation
A broken culture has taught

To be free of Earth time
What does that mean for us now?
Living moment to moment
Without the whys or the hows

Two hearts drifting in space
Balloons bursting with love
That just go where they blow
In the forever now
Is enough.

Earthquake

Off guard you hit my life like an earthquake
Shaking my deepest foundations to the core
Ripping open illusions of rock beneath my feet
Emotional tsunamis breaking down invisible walls

Fires of Hell consuming rage in the darkness
Hearts breaking free from the destruction of fear
Illuminating visions of planting orchards of love
Flowers blossoming through the tracks of my tears

An impact so deep it makes no difference
If this moment lasts an instant or for eternity
Your shockwaves will be felt forever in my heart
Beating to the softest echoes of divine mystery.

Growing Pains

Everybody wants
Love to be easy
To awaken each day
With the joy flowing freely

But love, like any skill
Needs to be learnt
Needs to be practised
Needs to be heard

What we tend to forget is
Through challenges we grow
Our journey goes within
I am not here to please you

Turn control into surrender
Resistance into flow
Acceptance comes with trust
Vulnerability safely grows

The divine irony is
In the end love is easy
Once the lessons have been learnt
And hearts are beating freely.

Fuck You

Fuck your fancy clothes and empty words
For they will never fill the space
Invite me to swim in the depths of your soul
And gift me your heart on a stake.

Show me stars instead of diamonds
Take me diving in your love
Fly me over the rainbow of sweet surrender
Forever lost in the Heavens above.

Heart Script

You came to me in a dream last night
I looked away, I had nothing to say
Done with your games and your sweet little lies
Best you leave 'cos I ain't here to play

But dreams have a habit of ignoring the mind
Leaving the heart to write its own script
Next thing I knew I was back in your arms
Forever lost where only love can exist.

Human Touch

You say
Time doesn't exist
And that distance is all in the mind
Yet I can't taste the truth on your lips
Or feel the strength of your arms
Wrapped in mine

Tell me
Who's going to hold me so tight
Every night as I'm falling asleep
And who am I kissing good morning
Each day as our sweet love
Is dawning

I'm here
Longing to touch Heaven on Earth
By getting lost in the depths of your eyes
Craving to smell the warmth of your skin
Making love to my breath
Of desire

I know
Our souls come from the stars
Divinely as one we are never apart
But I need to feel this human experience
Hearing sacred beats with my head
On your heart.

Sweet Dreams

Baby I'm missing you tonight
Thoughts of you stealing my sleep
Longing to feel your arms around me
To smell our love upon the sheets

Wings carrying me over the oceans
Laying me down gently by your side
Basking here sleepily in your glory
Embraced in love I close my eyes

Bird song heralding the morning
My heart recalling where I've been
Was I dreaming you were real?
Or were you really in my dreams?

Inferno

That feeling
That yearning
That burning in my heart
Heaven lit on fire
Blazing through our thoughts

Each one of us a flame
Dancing in the great fire of love
Freedom of expression
Divinity channelled from above

Fire raging with passion
Flames illuminate and rise
Sizzling, sparkling
Searing heat inside

Some will scar
Some will die
And slowly turn out their light
As the inferno of love
Seeks to cremate what we fight

From ashes
Flames rise once more
With the power of a spark
As the gentle touch of love
Ignites light from the dark.

Mermaid Blues

Feeling
Unseen
Unheard
Unacknowledged
Ignored

The deepest cut
The twisting pain
The wrenching violation
Of her human heart

Ebbing
Cruel resistance
To the flow of Divinity

Blindly
Swimming alone
In the ocean of consciousness

Drowning
In her tears of unawareness
That we are one.

Oceans Apart

I've decided I'll keep you
It took me a while
But I can no longer resist
That wanton look in your eyes
Strutting into my heart
Like you always belonged
Melting my stubborn insistence
That we were all wrong

You see I'd asked for a lover
Arms to hold me at night
Breath to tickle my neck
Lips to kiss at first light
One to rise with in love
To dive deeper together
A strong hand I could hold
Up the freeway to Heaven

And so what did I get
For my well thought out plans?
But an ocean of struggle
Between me and my man
Yet the wizard he worked
His sweet magic on me
Whispering spells in my ear
Till he set my heart free

Fearlessly riding the waves
Through the depths of my heart
Lighting inward reflections
So I could see in the dark
Together we had to let go
To surrender boldly to love
To trust drowning in faith
To know the ocean is us.

Sun Dance

His love was her reason
For awakening each dawn
Entwined rising together
Another new day is born

Sun's gift for his beloved Gaia
Infinite light from his heart
Divine contracts are honoured
Promises to never drift apart

Safely embraced in his arms
Passion ablaze with sacred fire
Kisses leading to Heaven
Surrender to flames of desire

One bleak morning she awoke
From sleeping under the stars
No longer sensing his glow
Crushing ache in her heart

Searching blindly through the fog
She sought his face in the sky
Feeling abandoned without him
Inner storms breaking to cry

Stumbling lost in the darkness
Amidst black clouds of her fears
Her body trembling with thunder
Rain drenched her with tears

Peeping out from the rainbow
The Sun's laugh was divine
I'm always here by your side
Those clouds are all in your mind.

Restless

She was a wild restless spirit
Amongst the stars, yet alone
Lost in the solitude of the storm
Recklessly seeking her way home

The wind invited her to dance
So she howled through the trees
Ferociously shaking every leaf
Becoming one with the breeze

The ocean challenged her to dive
So she sank into its depths
Emotions crashing against rocks
Becoming one with the waves

Her heart exhausted from the fight
Finally surrendered to the flow
The current took her in his arms
Whispers of peace began to blow

As she gazed into his eyes
She saw the reflection of the road
Home is not a place you seek
More the direction to your soul.

War

Eyes locked across the battlefield
Fearlessly sizing each other up
The greatest foes of all time
Fighting for her love

Since the beginning of forever
They'd drawn their bloody swords
Defiantly vying once again
Through the echoes of her thoughts

The mind in conflict with the heart
Only one could ever win
To claim the victory of her soul
And enter Paradise within

The duel for love is never easy
But the pain is oh so sweet
The salvation of surrender
Triumphantly swept her off her feet

Her gallant hero was declared
The bravest warrior won the war
Jubilantly lifting her in his arms
To claim his heavenly rewards.

Part 4
Breaking

He had always
Wanted her
To be free
So
She let him
Go.

Act of Faith

Defiantly she kept on fighting
Until eventually
He forced her up against the wall
Holding the butcher's knife to her throat

After years of war
This was the moment she surrendered
To whatever
Quietly accepting her fate

And that single act of faith
That trust in a higher power
That fearless indifference to life or death
Gently put her in the flow

The flow of least resistance
Where the ocean of peace
Lovingly took her in his arms
And carried her home.

Blessings

I loved you the way
I always hoped love to be
True to the heart
Open and deep

My gift was my heart
It was all yours to take
You took it and loved it
Didn't want it to break

Laughter and joy
Gratitude and tears
Surrendering to trust
Choosing love over fear

You had your sweet reasons
For doing as you did
No expectations we'd promised
So I accept what was said

To share love for a day
Is to feel such Divine presence
So the many we shared
Heartfelt heavenly blessings

Hearts can be broken
But true love can never break
A connection like ours
Will always yearn to re-awake.

Earth Bound

Sometimes she cries
Without knowing why
Bound within the mind
Of Earthly space and time
Yearning for the call
To return to the stars
That faraway place
Still alive in her heart

The hunger is real
To dissolve into love
Enough of this world
And its dark, heavy blood
She aches to fly free
Back to her natural state
Beyond feeling the pain
That her human creates

Tired of this life
And the darkness it brings
Seeking her truth
With the joy that it sings
Songs from her homeland
Now starting to flow
Her tears filling the river
To carry her home.

Slaughterhouse

Dancing in the rain
So he wouldn't taste her tears
Blinded by his smile
So she couldn't see his fears

Pumping up the music
Until she silenced her own cries
Singing his sweet words
Till she forgot about the lies

Isn't life just perfect?
He whispered, tightening her chains
Welding her heart back together
With the seduction of his flames

As she slowly closed the curtains
Across the window of her pain
To pay the ransom of their dream
Her soul was slaughtered once again.

Your Journey

They don't want to share your journey
Their shadows lengthen in your light
To be rejected for being you
Is a mountain you must climb

Their fears will hate you and forsake you
Say your heart is telling lies
So you listen to the beat within
To the truth you hear inside

It's saying to be faithful
To yourself and to your dreams
The love you seek is there within
Go claim and set it free

The road to love is a lonely one
Which must be walked alone
It's the only way you'll face yourself
And see the beauty you behold.

Empty Castles

So you got your fancy mansion
Golden dream house by the sea
Overlooking Heaven's playground
The promise of joy eternally

That's the illusion sold right there
I know it's hard for you to see
While you are caged up in your office
With concrete views for company

Banks yanking on your chains
Continual crashing waves of fear
Time traded with your soul
For lures of false security

Sand squishing between my toes
Warm breeze kissing salty lips
I'm here living out your dream
Moments you will forever miss

Dancing my footprints on the beach
Lined with empty castles by the sea
While you pay the price of Heaven
By dying in the hell of your reality.

Slam

You turned and walked away
And decided not to feel
The risk of pain, was it too great?
The depth of love we shared too real?

I felt you slam the door
Retreating safe into your mind
Your heart shutting out our love
Were you afraid what you might find?

I still feel your heart's desires
Because it speaks its truth to mine
Softly whispering that your love
Is locked away now deep inside

Time will slowly cut the key
Reigniting love to light the sky
Opening hearts to live to freedom
Unleashing your angel wings to fly.

Last Dance

As the music slows down
And the lights start to dim
The last song of the night
Stirs the embers within

As our eyes meet in love
For the very last dance
The heat of our touch
Recalls the thrill of romance

As the curtain falls down
And we take our final bow
The love lit in our hearts
Will forever burn in the now.

Light Girl

They sensed she was different
Not one of their crowd
So they gathered their knives
Laced with venom and bile

She was just a young girl
When they hacked off her wings
Locking her voice in a cage
Gagging all impulse to sing

Stabbing their hate in her back
Chaining her freedom with fear
Wounds etched deep in a planet
Trembling with oceans of tears

A little light girl on Earth
Shining love from the stars
Sadly blew out her flames
And closed the door to her heart.

Burn Baby Burn

She begged him for Heaven
So he sent her to Hell
To dig her way out of
The pits where she fell

Raging in the darkness
She screamed for a light
A flicker of hope
To enlighten the night

Hearing her plea
He threw her a flame
Burn baby burn
Torment in your pain

Surrendering to the silence
She was led by her heart
The gift is the fire
What you see in the dark

Embracing the inferno
To illuminate not scorch
She beheld the beauty of Heaven
She'd just needed a torch.

Rendezvous

Tomorrow you go journeying
Off into your heart
Letting go of my hand
Drifting further apart

We'll send our love letters
To the dimensions above
And rendezvous upon stars
Amidst vibrations of love

So breathe into this moment
And connect with me here
Breathe into our love
We have nothing to fear

I feel your heart beating
To the rhythm of mine
Divinity rising together
Throughout space and time

This love I am feeling
Is not of this Earth
Forever lost in our Heaven
Awaiting joyous rebirth.

Shattered

All those years ago
I used to ask myself,
Why do you stay?

I stay because I love him.

As an older, wiser version of myself
I can now gently tell that shattered woman

No, my dear,
You don't stay because you love him,
You stay because you do not love yourself.

Wild Hearts

Did you shut down your heart
To protect me from love?
Or have you locked yourself in
To forget about us?

Are you afraid of getting lost
In the depths of my eyes?
Or losing sight of your dreams
If we both learn to fly?

But our love cannot be chained
Wild hearts yearn to run free
Free to love who they want
And to love as they please

Your mind ahead in tomorrows
Future light years away
While love lives in the now
And my heart is open today.

Part 5
Breathing

Each day
An intention
Inspired from above
A little less me
A little more love.

Barefoot Angel

She makes love to the world
Through the soles of her feet
Feeling the rhythm of life
In every step that she greets

Deep conversations with Gaia
Love kissing the dirt
Barefoot angel from Heaven
Her feet gracing Mother Earth.

Cosmos

Can you see what I see
When I look into your eyes?
The magnificence of the Universe
Cascading galaxies in the sky

Jewels that shine like diamonds
Through the darkness of the night
Rainbow shades of stardust
Reflecting back the light

Soaring high up with the Angels
Surrendering to torrents of desire
Feeling the beating of your heart
Burning our own eternal fire

Enchanted worlds of discovery
Hiding the gateway to your soul
The heavenly glory of divinity
Soon unravelling as our own

Now take my hand I'll show you
Earth's most coveted surprise
Just gaze into the mirror my love
And see the cosmos in your eyes.

New Moon

We all behold the divine power
The magic to change our world
Whatever we give our energy to stays
Things we stop thinking about
Slowly begin to fade away

This is how we shift vibrationally
Aligning with different realities
Seeing the world through our real eyes
Each unfolding moment at a time
Creating truth where our thinking lies

Feelings give magnitude to thoughts
Spoken words amplify and reinforce
The magic is already within us
Potent energy in our minds
The power of love within our hearts.

Dance

Alive in the dream
It is what it is
Persistent illusion
Appearing as fact

But go deep within
And create what you feel
Emotions come from the heart
Only feelings are real

You see we live in a world
Where yesterday is a lie
Time and distance don't exist
And tomorrow never arrives

You can have what you want
Just feel it inside
Dance to the music
And hang on for the ride.

Breathing Love

I had to let you go
To be released from Earthly time
No more attachments to tomorrow
Now free to spread my wings and fly

The bliss of soaring in a world
Where only love is what we breathe
Flowers humming sacred tunes
Heaven dancing through the trees

Maybe it's here we'll meet again
Beneath the rainbow of our dreams
Amidst a shower of cosmic rays
Drinking bubbly moonshine beams

Love only lives here in the now
And now I'm free to love again
To live this moment as forever
Breathing love in Earth's new reign.

Just Breathe

With her feet grounded
Firmly within the Earth
She was nourished
And given the love of the planet

With her eyes gazing trustingly
Towards the Heavens
She was illuminated
And given the light of the stars

And with her hands placed
Gently upon her heart
She was thankful
And given the wisdom of the Universe.

Ocean of Soul

The ocean of soul
Laps upon every shore
Each wave is unique
As individuals are formed

We believe we are separate
A wave walking alone
But how is that possible
When the ocean is one?

We breathe on this Earth
In our physical form
Living blind to the truth
Of our connection to all

The ocean she rises
To greet each new birth
Gently welcoming us home
When on death we return.

First Kiss

The first kiss
The last dance
Duets of heartbeats
In between

Love never counts
Each time we breathe
But counts each breath
Between the times.

Power

They've got you on the treadmill
Running so fast you cannot stop
Malignant cycle to consume
Of debt and work and lack

Free press spends your money
Dictates beliefs and how to feel
Propaganda, fake news reports
Scripted opinion within the spiel

So you think that this is freedom
That you really have a choice
Blind to see a different reality
Deaf to your authentic voice

If you stop for just one moment
Sit out underneath the trees
Feeling the earth beneath your feet
Listening to whispers in the breeze

You will hear the call of home
Messages flowing from within
Directions to a life of freedom
Raising goose bumps on your skin

Ask questions, it tells no lies
The truth is loud and clear
Saying step into the world of love
Move away from hate and fear

Secret knowledge of the cosmos
Wisdom embodied from the stars
Hidden in silence is the truth
Just surrender to your heart.

Wings

Thoughts of you
Tiptoeing through my mind
Playing hide and seek
With my heart

Hearts can feel
What eyes cannot see
Love dancing its light
In the dark

Duets we sing
Music comes and it goes
Free to be here
Or afar

No strings attached
To a love like ours
None needed
For love of the heart.

Surrender

The path of least resistance
Is to just surrender and let it be
Allowing the tide to carry us out
Meeting the magnificence of the sea

For it is only when we let go of land
Releasing the fear within our grip
Hearts open up to receive the love
Flowing all around us infinitely

So be guided by the currents
True bliss of floating in the flow
Trusting Heaven is always within reach
Under the cascades of the rainbow.

Part 6
Healing

Crying your tears
From lifetimes gone by
The pain and the glory
Of knowing
We are one.

Bleeding Love

Love heals all wounds
And soothes the aching pain

Let me gently kiss your scars
Those etched deep within your heart

Until they fade away
Along with the memories of yesterday

For your wounds
Are only illusions

Thoughts bleeding love

Carving a gaping hole
In the perfection of your soul.

World of Love

Welcome to my world of love
Where rainbows fill the skies
Sweet sounds of colour everywhere
Painted rhythms come alive

Waterfalls flirting with delight
Moonbeams dancing through the trees
Rainclouds bursting tears of joy
Flowers kissing in the breeze

This world of love is there for all
Feel the truth within your heart
A light of hope when darkness hits
When you are lost amidst the stars

So take my hand, I'll lead you there
Right up to Heaven's shore
Then place your hands upon your heart
And feel the knocking on the door

You see my dear you are the one
Where Heaven meets the Earth
You hold the key to better dreams
Just see the love within your world.

Diamonds

Her tears they shone like diamonds
Through the darkness of the night
A million tiny mirrors
Reflecting back the light

She edged a little closer
Amazed by what she saw
The light within the darkness
Was her beauty after all.

Footprints

Salty lips and naked toes
Fresh footprints through her mind
As she thought about life's heartaches
And the way love ebbs and flows

Raw memories of his words
Building castles made from sand
Overnight the waves came crashing in
By morning he was gone

She closed her eyes and listened
To the wind whispering in her ear
Turn around it said, and look again
The sand is cleared from all your tears

Ocean love swiftly washing away
Blue memories from her heart
No longer here except in your mind
Embrace a brand new start

Waves cast their magic on the shore
Washing away tracks of the past
Reminding her that memories
Are only real when the mind looks back

So fill your thoughts with rainbows
To create your laughter for today
Feet leaving heartache in the sand
For waves to wash the pain away.

Hell's Gate

Walk through the forest to the valley of peace
Feel the silence breaking in every heart beat
Surrender drowning thoughts to the river of flow
Sprinkle misty tears where the sunflowers grow

Offer rising fears up to the mountains of joy
Heal painful wounds beneath the soothing rainbow
Release expectations to the wisdom of the trees
Free tomorrow's worries in the faraway breeze

Dance in the gardens where the bluebirds sing
Paint peaceful smiles onto butterfly wings
Follow love's path to the sanctuary of presence
Open your heart to step from Hell's gate to Heaven.

Dragons

Feel the spirit of the dragons
Let them lift you on their wings
Believe the secrets they are breathing
The peace their ancient wisdom brings

See the magic in their fire
Infusing light into your heart
Igniting the power to rise in love
Healing a world falling apart.

Map to Heaven

Start in Hell
Traverse the Forgiveness Mountains
Cross over the Victim River
Trek through the Forest of Attachment
Sail across the Ocean of Fear

If at any time you lose your way
Seek directions from the Valley of Silence
Be grateful for the signposts written with love
And be guided by the light of your heart.

Reflections

Suddenly I see you
For what you really are
Hidden aspects of me
I can no longer ignore

How can I not love
What I see in your eyes
The pure reflection of me
So divinely disguised

That day I walked away
To set myself free
Little did I know
I was running from me.

Gratitude

She graciously thanked the wolf
For abandoning her
For he had gifted her
Her strength

She proudly thanked the lioness
For rejecting her
For she had taught her
Her worth

And she silently thanked the beast
For hating her
For he had shown her
Her wings.

Scars

Hearts fill and burst
Then crack and break
They bleed and scar
Search love to make

Hearts ache and cry
With sacred tones
Sweet music heard
By us alone

And somewhere
In that star-filled sky
Stories are told
For reasons why

Our hearts are leaders
Of the pack
Follow their light
And bring love back.

Stepping Stones

Our path is lit with stepping stones
Leading up to an oasis of peace
Choosing the ones that open our hearts
We invite love to be released

Some days along our journey
Storm clouds will darken the skies
Afraid and unsure which step to take
We will stumble and wonder why

The light we seek to flood our path
Is right there inside our hearts
Just open the gates and free the love
To find the peace within your world.

Whispers

He told me
I wasn't the one
He told me
I wasn't enough
He told me
The light he'd seen in my eyes
Was no longer worthy of his love

Seeking answers from the Heavens
The wind blew away my tears
Whispering
In me he'd seen his image
His words reflecting his own fears.

Silent Release

She took a wrong turn
Down the River of Life
Swimming blindly upstream
Heading nowhere very fast

Clinging to rocky edges
Crushed by fallen trees
Battling raging torrents
Seduced by death's tease

She ached and she bled
Until her pain dragged her under
Silent release
As she finally surrendered

Her heart beating to freedom
Embracing love in the flow
Trusting deep Divine waters
Knew best where to go

Today peacefully floating
With her tomorrows adrift
Life is carrying her home
Down the River of Bliss.

Monsters

Licking bitter wounds of battle
She built a tower from her fear
Safely locked away her beauty
Behind a river cried from tears

But she couldn't escape the beast
For he lived inside her head
No amount of bricks and mortar
Could stop her demons being fed

Searching desperately for an exit
She found the doorway to her heart
Painting a rainbow of new truth
Light shining deep within the dark

The beast was not the enemy
It was the thoughts inside her mind
So she stripped her cloak of terror
Baring her soul to realign

She tamed her inner beast
Loving the monster she had feared
Seeing stars within the darkness
Grateful for the gift of every tear.

Wounded

I want you to lead me
To that place in your heart
Where no one has ventured
And that's where we'll start

Beginning a journey of healing
Through years of painful scars
Feeling the depths of raw truth
Kissing our tears as they fall

For only love holds the power
To heal every open wound
Your bleeding pain is my mirror
I am the broken image of you.

Part 7
Rising

Where will I meet you?
he asked her.
In the now,
she replied.
For that is where love is.

Cocooned

Aching and defeated
She left for good that day
Bleeding from the battles
And the lies he'd made her play

Picking up her broken heart
She tearfully blew out the light
Wrapped it up in darkness
And surrendered to the night

The cocoon was warm and cosy
Protection from love's dangers
The only thing that gave her strength
Were the smiles of her two Angels

As the light began to filter in
She saw the beauty of her scars
Igniting the greatest power of all
Burning love within her heart

Claiming victory from the battlefield
So much wiser for her blessings
The once fearful little caterpillar
Woke up and stretched her wings.

Flowers

The sun peeped through the curtains
A new dawn had just begun
Reminding her of flowers
And the battles she had won

The pain that she had planted
And watered with her tears
Now a blossoming garden of love
To be shared instead of feared.

Home

Her heart it was his sanctuary
From the cold, dark world outside
His little piece of Paradise
Fuelled with sacred love on fire

Gazing wistfully at the moon
She recalled the night he'd walked away
Knowing he'd pocketed the key
Certain to need it again someday

She could feel that he was homesick
For her heart began to dance
Hearing him whispering her name
Igniting sparks of sweet romance

With stars shining on the road ahead
He saw gates to Heaven in her eyes
Honoured to be the only man
Who held the key to step inside

Jumping back into his arms
The blaze of fire began to roar
For home is where the hearth is
Flames burning love forever more.

Shine

It's the moment to get naked
The time has come for us to shine
To go and strip off all those people
Who are still weighing us down

Those diminishing our successes
Who refuse to share our joys
Wanting to shove us in a box
Feeling threatened as we grow

Those who try to dim our light
Those who think they know it all
Those who live in fear of love
Those who are afraid to fall

Together rising in our truth
Gaia needs our shining light
Healing time is always now
And the moment's oh so ripe

To fling our hearts wide open
Freeing the abundance of our souls
Dancing to the rhythm of our love
Rejoicing with Earth as she glows.

Presents

You see the thing about love
Is that it's never ours to keep
Gifts shared in sacred moments
With every breath and each heartbeat

Once the moments disappear
We return back to the start
To our heavenly anticipation
Of receiving presence from the heart.

Earth Angels

The Earth cried tears of rivers
Terror shaking deep within her core
Fire raged like molten anger
Tempests ravaged every shore

Saddened and defeated
Knowing her darkest day was near
She gasped the last breath of her forests
And made her desperate plea

Then twinkling across the darkened sky
She beheld millions of lights
Each one love burning in the hearts
Of Earth Angels putting up a fight

Dawn sky lit up with shooting stars
Sun cracking open all the flowers
Rainbows painting tears of joy
Love rejoicing in her finest hour.

Rainbow Wings

Butterflies laughing in the breeze
Dancing high above the waves
Singing it's time for you to fly
Your world can never be the same

They told me of their stories
Of how far they had all come
When as larvae they were birthed
And their misery had just begun

They spoke of far-off galaxies
And of stars from outer space
Their incarnation onto Gaia
The painful heartbreak that took place

They told me of the darkness
How they feared the end was near
Doomed as lifeless little caterpillars
They lay drowning in their tears

Did they cross the veil of reason?
Or rise to dimensions filled with love?
Were they still on planet Earth?
Or peering down from up above?

Were they soaring with the Angels?
Or creating magic from the ground?
Spreading wings of rainbow colours
Music lifting them with sound

The darkness was their saviour
As they surrendered to their plight
Now here soaring with the ocean
Rejoicing in heavenly delight.

Lead Me Home

I love you
But I don't need you
Holding your hand
Or walking alone

Journeying to Heaven
With or without you
Following my heart
To lead me home.

Rising in Love

We have come to heal the planet
In her desperate time of need
Bringing light to lift the darkness
Soothing the pain as she bleeds

Feeding love into her veins
We are spread across the globe
Knowing we have a sacred mission
Memories starting to unfold

Time for hearts to come together
And free humanity from control
Chains of fear breaking open
Liberty starting to unroll

Let's join hands and lift our Earth
Out of the depths of her despair
Rising up to claim our freedom
The power of love changing the air.

Sacred Dawn

Painting sunrises of hope
Across fresh skies
Birthing golden promises
Of a brand new year
When the glory of love
Will triumphantly rise
Lifting up the veil
From Earth's darkest fears

Light exposing shadows
Lurking in deception
Our Gaia rising up
Defiantly from her knees
Hearts melting ice
After bleak days of winter
Sacred dawn thawing
The bitter age of tears

Orchards of blossoms
Singing in the sunshine
Humanity awakening
Freed from lives of pain
Hearts beating change
To rhythms of ascension
Anticipation dancing
As the truth of love reigns.

Honey

Today the devil swung on by
To trade a piece of my soul
Demanding I sell out my truth
So she could pay me with gold

Disguised as the angel of joy
Selling dreams to empty hearts
Dripping honey to the needy
Gluing visions ripped apart

But I have nothing here to sell
For true love cannot be bought
A river flowing deep within me
Loosely held but never caught

Love abounds here in the present
A priceless gift don't you see
Power to light a darkened world
Can only be given away for free.

Steps to Heaven

Climbing the stairway to Heaven
Is no easy feat
Loving reflections of us
In every person we meet

Each step is a love story
Engraved into time
The pain and the glory
From darkness we rise

We love
We fear
We break
We heal

We feel
We love
We rise

One step closer to Heaven
Repeat.

Part 8
Divine Feminine

Love slowly revealing
Who I really am
A beautiful reminder
Of how far I have come.

Angels

Glaring through darkened glasses
Blinded by the light
I hate your smile, the Bitch yelled out
You're shining way too bright

The Angel didn't falter
She'd seen it all before
She knew the pain was telling lies
And building up a wall

She took her gently by the hand
And removed her cloak of fear
You see your wings were always here
Just hidden by your tears

She bathed the Bitch's bleeding wings
Stitched up her broken heart
Straightened up her halo
And kissed her painful scars

She led her to the edge of glory
And said a fond goodbye
For Bitches are only Angels
Who have yet to learn to fly.

Wild Women Warriors

Wild women warriors
Fearlessly rising up on Earth
Declaring the divinity of our power
Reclaiming the birth right of our worth

Healing wounds upon the planet
Wisdom gained through tears of blood
Wearing battle scars like diamonds
Alchemy of fear into love

Softly illuminating the darkness
Stitching the hearts of broken souls
Uplifting the fallen with our kindness
Guiding those lost along the road

A blazing flare we stand together
Reflecting the brightness of the stars
For those walking the sacred journey
From their heads into their hearts.

Goddess

Trust the wild beating of your heart
Resist the fear that's ripped you apart
Unbolt the doors of your fortified tower
Feel the raw trembling of your power

Walk like a goddess into his arms
Submit to the seduction of his charms
Hear sweet angels singing above
Surrender and be claimed by love.

She

She was the echo whispering his name from the Heavens
She was the storm creating chaos in his heart
She was the wind calling him to dive into her ocean
She was the fire burning desire within his soul

She was the thunder demanding his surrender in the silence
She was the sunset painting rainbows across the skies
She was the moon hiding her dark side in the shadows
She was the stars reflecting beauty in his eyes

She was the rain dripping sweat down his torso
She was the iceberg sending shivers up his spine
She was the volcano erupting passion in the darkness
She was the earthquake raising goose bumps in his mind

She was the dawn stirring his senses in the morning
She was the breeze running her fingers through his hair
She was the dew kissing his lips between the laughter
She was the sun caressing his skin with her flare

She was the Earth making love to all his senses
She was the sense he was love making on Earth
She was the air breathing life into his body
All he knew was that he had to breathe again.

My Love

It was always you
My love
But I was hurting
And I was closed
Too blinded by pain
To know

To see you
To feel you
To trust you
To touch you

I travelled the planet
I explored the stars
Searching relentlessly
In the eyes
Of every past lover
For you

And now
I have found you
Where you were all along
Waiting in the depths
Of my darkest chambers

I found you in my surrender
I feel you in my peace
I know you in my trust
I touch you in my love

You were always here
Waiting so patiently
For me to find myself
To finally shine my light
And open the portal
To my heart.

Perfect Chaos

She knows that she's not perfect
And she no longer tries to be
Divine imperfections of Gaia herself
Expressed in her glorious mess

Feeling as deeply as the forests
Emotions swaying in the breeze
Storm clouds raging with her thunder
Her heartbeat aching to fly free

She's as twisted as the mountains
Wildfire threatening in every breath
Embodying the chaos of Mother Nature
Creating the balance of life itself.

Girl on the Cliff

So here I am standing
On the cliff once again
Cold wind chilling my bones
Memories stabbing their pain

How many lives have I stood
On this very same spot?
Sailors come and then go
Will they stay, will they not?

The wound bleeds so deep
In the feminine heart
Broken promises of love
Sacred dreams ripped apart

Waiting here on the cliff
For his return from the sea
While fear aches to remember
That love lives inside me.

Wave of Love

She saw the wave approaching
What was a girl to do?
With every high that'd come before
She'd crashed into the rocks

She drew a fearless breath
Resolved her strength of mind
Refusing to feed the dangers
Surrendering each moment at a time

The swell swept her off her feet
She was lifted high towards the sky
The edge of glory was here and now
The choice was hers to find

If she energised the fear
She knew that she would fall
So instead she felt within her heart
To hear her guidance call

As the wave uncurled its power
She slipped into the stream
Riding every golden moment
Exhilarated in the dream

In the whitewash of the aftermath
She gasped, enthralled by the ride
Ready for the next wave of love
To lift her to Paradise.

Enchanted

The birds woke her with their laughter
Broadcasting the news of the day
She listened spellbound by their chatter
And smiled watching them play

At one here with the forest
Sunshine dancing through the leaves
The ancient wisdom of the Elders
Embodied deep within the trees

She could feel her heart was thumping
Drumming to the music of her soul
The enchanting magic of the spirits
Whispering stories to unfold

Forever grateful for the honour
To witness such Heavenly joy and peace
Knowing she'd found Paradise on Earth
By allowing love to be released.

Woman

Woman you are the ocean
Fearlessly surging to new heights
Birthing eternal waves of thunder
Shimmering softly in your light

Rising defiantly in your glory
Crashing broken to your depths
Shifting awareness in the waters
Creating life with every breath

Seduction flirting with the darkness
Sunshine kissing salty tears
Surrendering wildly in your passion
Emotions dancing on the breeze

Reflecting silence in the moonlight
Seeking wisdom from the stars
Swirling struggle in your torrents
Nourishing Gaia with your heart

Drenching fear with loving ripples
Gracefully lapping every shore
Shaping rock with flowing softness
Claiming the power to change your world.

Part 9
Divine Masculine

.

Wrenching open his heart
She drew blood from his scars
Surrender
Is the sweetest pain.

Au Revoir

She recalled the last time
He'd looked into her eyes.
She knew he'd recognised
The infinite depths of his own soul.
Reflecting a source of truth
That could only have come
From Heaven itself.

It left him with nowhere to hide
But back into his own heart
To discover his journey
And find his way back to her.

Heart Warrior

After endless lifetimes
Fighting heartless wars
The time has come
For our brave warriors
To lay down their weapons

For the battle between
Heart and ego
The noble fight for
Peace and freedom

Can only be won
By surrendering...
To the power of love.

Ego

So
You've released all your attachments
Say you've nothing left to fear
No longer dancing with your ego
Confident the road ahead is clear

You've got this being human sorted
And know all there is to know
Defiantly arrogant in your glory
Feeling smug within your flow

You've ticked and checked your boxes
Climbed the ladder to success
As if your journey has an end
Placing you way above the rest

But can you strip down your defences?
Revealing your weakness to the world?
Kneeling vulnerably in your nakedness?
Grateful for the pain as it unfurls?

Thoughts of you crossing my mind
Dear men I've met over the years
Ego harshly judging those I see?
Or merely reflecting my own fears?

Diving deep into our infinity
Surrendering to love to heal our minds
Let's travel the road to Paradise together
As humble equals side by side

Heaven's door is open for all
Not just those who pass the test
We're each as perfect as each other
And every heart divinely blessed.

Feathers

Feathers floating through the window
Resting gently on the bed
As he wrapped his wings around her
She lay her head upon his chest

He hadn't come to save her
Or protect her from her fears
Nor as an answer to her prayers
Or to wipe away her tears

A human angel here on Earth
Feeling her vibration from afar
He'd come to share his loving grace
And return to Heaven through her heart.

Weary Warrior

Come home my weary warrior
Come back home into your heart
Enough fighting earthly demons
Writing history with your scars

How many lifetimes have I waited
To hear love beat inside your chest
To see truth shining in your freedom
To feel real warmth in your caress

Sweet home is where your heart is
Where you live when love flies free
Your surrender is your strength
Come on home now
Back to me.

Masculine Wound

He's too scared to love
But so tired of the fight
Raw pain of our masculine
Disarming his plight

The first shot was fired
At his moment of birth
Flung from feminine love
Into a world raging war

Every woman has paid
For that cruel separation
As he shut down his heart
Blaming her in damnation

Dear men, cry your tears
Feel now your true mission
You came here in peace
In your hearts it is written

Forgive your dear mother
For honouring your choice
To deliver you on Earth
As sweet angels rejoiced

She loved you as deeply
As she could at that time
It was never her fault
You did not stay inside

Let me hold you, surrender
Welcome trust once again
Divine union of love
Comes as faith is regained.

Surrender to Love

Still hurting and bloodied
He returned home from war
Another human heart broken
Crushed in conflicts he'd fought
Angry pain digging deeper
Than a man knew how to feel
Violence erupting in wounds
A severed mind can never heal

A flesh soldier over lifetimes
Conditioned to kill and defeat
Programmed to die as a hero
For his land of forced beliefs
Firing weapons of hatred
From behind walls in his heart
Hiding his masculine virtue
Under a society ripped apart

But you are home now dear warrior
Come lay your head on my heart
As I gently stitch up your wounds
And kiss better each scar
Time to remember your mission
Your sacred calling from above
All your wars will be over
When you surrender to love.

Wolf Love

Scars etched from bloody battles
Fearlessly defiant against the pack
Lone wolf turned from fighting chaos
Knew he was never going back

Instincts driven by fierce love
Rising reborn from lives of pain
No longer trapped inside the beast
Wilderness refusing to be tamed

Risking life to change his world
Howls piercing silence in the breeze
Alone yet stronger than before
Wild beauty yearning to run free

Solitude dancing with the devil
Hunting truth across new land
Seeking a mate to join in union
To make sweet love under the moon

Slinking paw prints melting snow
The king prowled to find his queen
Two spirits hungry for the fire
Her heart surrendered to his lure

Divinity opening Heaven's door
Freedom aching to give birth
Together as one in sacred love
Territory claimed upon New Earth.

Part 10
Sacred Union

Flowing with presence
Stillness in movement
For she was his ocean
And he was her rock.

Battle Cry

She's yearning for connection
He's seeking to fly free
Eyes locked on the dance floor
Love's battle-cry released

He pushes and she pulls
She craves to feel him near
He retreats creating space
She learns to trust his lead

He ebbs just like the tide
She flows to fill the void
Hearts beating harmonised
In freedom they are joined

She guides him to his heart
He directs her to her worth
Both dancing now as one
Sacred music on New Earth

Divine power in the dance
Love's balance to just be
Together in their distance
Unified yet flowing free

As the music starts to slow
She lets go of his hand
Giving him freedom to fly free
Knowing he will always
Fly back home.

Lightning Bolt

The sudden, electrifying jolt of my heart
Brings me crashing back down to Earth
Awakened from my deepest dreams

I listen in awe as the thumping
Echoes through the silence of the night,
Feeling every vibration
As it ripples through my quivering body.

Have your thoughts turned to me again?
Is your soul calling to mine in mutual surrender?
I wonder what force could ignite
Such a powerful response from my tender heart.

Deep within I already know the answer…
Only a lightning bolt of love
Sent straight from your heart.

Bold Demand

A woman knows
When her man has truly
Opened his heart
Just by the look in his eyes

It's this humble power of masculine
Presence and vulnerability
This bold demand
That she lay down her defences
And trust him to lead her

That leaves her no choice...
But to surrender fully into love.

Edge of Heaven

Gently taking her by the hand
He led her to the edge of the cliff
The waters he was inviting her to dive into
Were not of this planet
Or even this dimension
Before them lay an infinite expanse
Of unchartered territory
The journey to discover Heaven itself

Gazing into his eyes
She recognised the ocean of love
Where waves of emotion
Rise and fall
To the silent symphony of their hearts

Depths
Where the fear of falling
Is seen only as a heavenly portal
To diving deeper into love.

Higher Love

It feels different this time
Not the same as before
Doesn't mean love is less
I'm still starting to fall

Together but detached
Nothing left to resist
Ocean flowing between us
Where no time exists

No thoughts of tomorrow
Nor memories gone by
Love lingering here now
Holding hands or alone

So this is how angels fly
When hearts open to sing
Lifting us higher on love
Freedom soaring on wings.

Drowning

So you want to dive into her ocean
To get lost in the depths of her soul
Tasting kisses leading to Heaven
Blazing love lighting up the road

It will not be the easiest journey
But one so much worth your pain
The blessed union of sacred hearts
Beating together as planned once again

Light sparkling at the top of her ocean
Will shimmer and invite you to swim
Joyful splashing and laughter in sunshine
Love smiling and growing within

Then as you sink into her waters
She will drown you so sweetly with love
Her light shining in corners of darkness
Stripping you naked with no place to run

It is here you are faced with two choices
Rise again to the surface and breathe
Or surrender to the currents of destiny
Allowing the power of love to lead

So keep diving deeper brave warrior
Priceless treasures are buried nearby
For her gallant hero with the courage
To wrench open his heart and find.

His Gift

He wanted her naked heart
So he gave her a gift
A gift that no man
Had ever given her before...

She wanted his naked heart
So he gave her a gift
A gift that no man
Had ever given her before...

The freedom
To be
Herself.

Immaculate Conception

I see the wonders in you
Of how I want me to be
Masculine strong in his truth
Thoughts expressed easily

Maybe you see in me
Of how you want you to be
Feminine dancing with love
Emotions flowing and free

Let's ignite within each
Hidden parts of the other
The inner, the outer
The father, the mother

Two wholes become three
As we rise birthing glory
Immaculate conception
The real human love story.

Naked

I yearn to love you as you are
In your purest state of Self
Sinking deeper through your layers
Undressing your authentic wealth

I crave your naked heart and soul
Baring all you have inside
To know you stripped of all your ego
Till I can taste your raw design

I want your passion
Your desire
For the me I give to you
Standing vulnerably as your mirror
The power of trembling in our truth

Of you I ask for nothing more
Than to be exactly who you are
So I can see in your reflection
Divinity flowing
Through my heart.

Wildfire

The kindling was dry
In the depths of his soul
A hollow, weary ache
Stone cold and alone

Her smouldering beauty
Sparked the thrill of desire
Wildfire swept through him
Setting the heavens on fire

An explosion of passion
Sizzling heat in the night
The dance of the flames
Engulfed by the light

She melted his heart
With the sweetest of sighs
Then sent him to Hell
With the glare in her eyes

Her warm touch caressed him
He fell asleep in her arms
Woken by a raging inferno
Firing bullets in his heart

Shivering with fever
He surrendered to the burn
For he could never extinguish
A wildfire like her.

Sweet Mercy

Oh you can try to control
This divine love we have found
Dipping your toes in the water
Afraid to dive in and drown

But flames cannot be bound
Or locked up in chains
Nor kept out at arm's length
To avoid feeling the pain

So how hungry is your thirst
For this rapture of the heart?
On a slippery slope to Heaven
Your world about to fall apart

Can you abandon all control?
Gift your heart upon a stake?
Risk losing everything for love?
Do whatever the hell it takes?

Whispers echoing in the silence
Pleading to satisfy the yearn
Igniting fire within your soul
Till you surrender to the burn

Your heart is aching to run wild
Power can never be contained
Hear it begging for sweet mercy
To feel my love without restraint.

Tango

The electrifying jolt of my heart
Brings me crashing back down to Earth
Awakened from my deepest dreams
I know you have come to dance

Echoing soulfully through the silence
Listening mesmerised by the beat
My body trembling to the rhythm
Of lovers fusing in the heat

Stardust sparkling on the dance floor
Blue moon shining its soft light
Shattered illusions of distance between us
Flames igniting passion in the tango of life.

Welcome Inside

I woke up feeling
Your hands on my body
Exploring my curves
Seeking to enter inside

But you are already here
You've been here forever
Always inside my heart
Slowly losing your mind

Touching my essence
Yearning to know us
Craving our union
Burning sacred desire

Now you have found me
You have my body
My heart is wide open
Welcome inside.

Part 11
And Then I Met You

In this world
With no labels
I will tie
Only one
We are lovers
That is all
For we are love.

Ancient Tears

I can feel your heart beating
Whispering its secrets to mine
Your memoirs are breathing
Scars from galaxies gone by

Ancient tears held in reverence
Trickling down human cheeks
Sorrow etched into heartache
Begging now to be released

Torment dissolves into love
When revered by such power
Wounds healed by our touch
Painful illusions unravelled

Suffering melted by light
No longer aching to be defined
Moments shared between lovers
Defying all space and time.

Eden

What if I told you
I won't break your heart
Now we've planted our seeds
Faith sprouts through the dark

What if I told you
I won't let you go
As we reach for our light
Trust allows love to grow

What if I told you
I know you're the one
Flowers opening our hearts
Impending glory begun

What if I told you
That you are in me
Our truth is now ripening
So delicious and sweet

What if I told you
Heaven's garden is us
Divine rapture in paradise
Reaping the fruits of our love.

Bridging Dimensions

In the 3 AM silence
Is when I hear you the loudest
Hearts beating wild passion
Sacred rhythms of love

Here alone in the darkness
I can I see you the brightest
Eyes shining as mirrors
Divine reflections of us

As I reach out to touch you
My body starts trembling
Your presence so strong now
Time and distance dissolved

Love bridging dimensions
Collapsing known timelines
Portals opening to Heaven
As above so below

Earthly cosmic encounters
Sprinkling stardust and wonder
Full galactic embodiment
Shooting light from the stars

Tantric chakras colliding
Oh the joy to be human
Igniting sensual rapture
Surrender safe in your arms

So does distance exist?
Or am I lost inside mind games?
Cruel illusions of space
Trapped in the matrix of time

But what does it matter
In the 4 AM silence
When I can drift back to sleep
With you now by my side.

Fragile Hearts

There was a tremor in her voice
As she looked him in the eyes
His face rough between her hands
Two fragile hearts collapsing time

My love, I know that it is you
The one I've waited lifetimes for
Tears softly rolling down her cheeks
Devils dancing through her thoughts

But you say don't dive too deep
Fearful words not from your heart
Her voice now fading to a whisper
Fresh blood painting ancient scars

Here we stand trembling as humans
Yet our souls come from the stars
Have you forgotten who is God?
Your light still tortured by the dark

So will you walk the edge of fear?
Like broken lovers before you
Men terrified to feel surrender
Grasping onto false control

Or bravely ride new heights to love?
Singing joy throughout the world
Stepping into human missions
To grace divinity upon New Earth

Let go my love, dive deep
Immerse in love and drown with me
Death bridging heavenly portals
Where sacred hearts can live freely.

Heartspeak

I tried to tell you that I love you
But my words got in the way
How can talking ever know
The truth my heart yearns to say

So come a little closer
Lay your head upon my breast
Feel the lyrics from my heart
To hear my love for you expressed.

Push My Buttons

Keep pushing my buttons Baby
As only you know how
Then push a little harder
Until my world turns upside down

Knot that aching in my belly
Rip scars open from the past
Feeling the human pain again
Of holding love within my grasp

Always there just out of reach
Here so close and yet so far
Desiring your scent upon my lips
Resisting the urge to fall apart

Then my heart begins to murmur
Whispering open up your hands
Stop gripping onto love so tightly
Release its power to expand

For we each need space to grow
To reach our highest state of bliss
Creating Heaven here on Earth
Where only us and love exist.

Insanity

Do not fall in love with me
You know that will mean trouble
I'll blow your mind
Waste precious time
Insanity is my promise

Do not fall in love with me
You know that means destruction
Ego naked
Fear seduced
Lips feeding your addiction

Do not fall in love with me
You know that means surrender
No more fighting
No more war
Love's victory will be humbling

Do not fall in love with me
You know that means redemption
You will rise up
A greater man
Love made in your perfection

Do not fall in love with me
You know that will mean Heaven
I'll burn with you
I'll melt with you
Love firing sweet obsession

But if you cannot help
Falling in love with me
Just know that means forever
Etched in my heart
Wrapped in your arms
Entwined as sacred lovers.

Quantum Love

Like attracts like
So before me you stand
My quantum reality
In the shape of a man

Strings entangled forever
Throughout space and time
Frequencies resonating as one
Vibrating heartbeats aligned

The illusion of you
The reality of me
Particles dancing together
Energy merging as we

Here united on Earth
As your skin kisses mine
Senses filled with your love
Heavenly bodies entwined.

No Limits

Some nights I miss you
A little more than others
I long to be in your bed
In the arms of my lover

My heart it can feel you
Defying all space and time
Where our love does the talking
Slowly losing my mind

Come meet me on Venus
Where no confines exist
Feel the warmth of my body
Quench my thirst with your lips

Lie down here beside me
Breathe in deep my desire
Feed my hunger for you
Light my heavenly fires

Take me soaring to places
Heights I've never yet seen
Push me higher in love
Transcending limitless dreams.

Sacred Dreams

Slipping back into sleep
I know you are here
My mind lost in your scent
Hearing your breathing so near

Together greeting the sunrise
Love awakening my spine
Portals opening to Heaven
Your kisses tasting divine

My body is trembling
As it melts into your fire
Inhaling each sacred breath
Surrendering earthly desires

Reality whispering its secrets
While making sweet love with you
Now can last forever
And dreams do come true.

Promised Land

If you're too afraid to fall in love
Then I will take you by the hand
Walk you through the veil of reason
On towards the Promised Land

Here we'll lie beneath the rainbow
And wait for you to catch your breath
Check for blood and broken bones
Ease the thumping in your chest

Then we'll find that sacred space
Somewhere deep behind your ribs
Where your love is locked away inside
Begging to be released

Your heart knows I hold the key
To unleashing all your wildest dreams
Bringing Heaven to your Earth
Setting your love forever free.

Stars Collide

You know how much I want you
To be squeezed tight in your arms
But you say that cannot be now
As we live on different stars

I'll wait because you're worth it
It's worth waiting for your charms
Meanwhile I'm gonna explore
Every crevice of your heart

So tell me all your secrets
What you think about in bed
When your mind is going crazy
When I'm stuck inside your head

Tell me all your dreams
Of how high you want to fly
Just make sure I'm flying with you
When we love our dreams alive

Tell me all your fears
Why your heart slams shut its door
Show me every darkened shadow
So I can see your light restore

For now we'll fly to far off galaxies
Meet for picnics on the moon
Practise telepathy over coffee
Bilocate and get a room

Because now you have found me
I'll always be here by your side
Just feel into your heart my love
It's where the two of us collide.

Rapture

Come let us dive deeper
To the depths of our souls
Past the ends of this earth
As our journey unfolds

Exploring the glory of you
Cosmic stardust in me
Entwined sacred in union
Touching divinity in we

Hearts surrendered to love
Gates opening to Heaven
Rainbows leading to now
Infinite celestial blessings

You are home now my lover
There is nothing to fear
True bliss is our birthright
Eternal rapture revealed.

Reunited

You saw me
I felt you
I invited you in

You opened me
You entered me
Our journey began

Deeper
And deeper
You filled me with love

Our rapture
Our heaven
The merging of us

Delighting
Exciting
Surrender to pain

An explosion of love
Hearts reunited
Once again.

CPSIA information can be obtained
at www.ICGtesting.com
Printed in the USA
LVHW050337261120
672644LV00013B/624

9 781528 904247